THE OFFICIAL CSPA STYLEBOOK

edited by Helen F. Smith

20th edition

Columbia Scholastic Press Association
Columbia University
CMR 5711
2960 Broadway
New York, N.Y. 10027-6902

THE OFFICIAL CSPA STYLEBOOK

INTRODUCTION

This stylebook is intended primarily for writers for student publications. It is the 20th successive edition of this publication issued by the Columbia Scholastic Press Association since the book's first appearance in 1928. More than 94,000 copies of the earlier editions have been printed.

The Association, an international organization, was founded in 1925 by Columbia University to serve the needs of student journalists in the United States, Canada and overseas schools.

To compile this edition of its stylebook, the Association turned to an experienced adviser, editor and author, Helen F. Smith. A graduate of Smith College, she has advised the *Newtonite* newspaper at Newton North High School, Newtonville, Mass., since 1973. During that period the *Newtonite* earned Gold Crown Awards, the Association's highest honor for a student publication, as well as other awards from the CSPA and several Gallup Awards from Quill and Scroll Society of the University of Iowa. She is the president of the Columbia Scholastic Press Advisers Association and executive director of the New England Scholastic Press Association. She has edited two editions of CSPA's *Scholastic Newspaper Fundamentals,* the 1988 edition of *The Official CSPA Stylebook* as well as the fifth edition of *Springboard to Journalism* and its accompanying *Teacher's Manual.* Since 1993 she has edited CSPA's *Student Press Review.* She received a Gold Key from the CSPA in 1987.

Grateful acknowledgment is given to Mike Hiestand, Esq., and the Student Press Law Center, Arlington, Va., for permission to use the essay on plagiarism beginning on page 71 and which originally was published in *Student Press Review.* Parts of this edition of this stylebook were excerpted or adapted from the *Newton North Writing Handbook*, edited by Helen F. Smith and published by the Newton Public Schools, 1995-96.

The suggestions made by this publication cover the points of usage most frequently encountered in student publications. No claim of originality or finality is made for this stylebook, but it is hoped that its use will result in better written and more uniformly edited student periodicals.

Edmund J. Sullivan
Director
Columbia Scholastic Press Association

A

a, an

Use the indefinite article, *a,* before consonant sounds: *a Halloween party, a 2005 model.*

Use the indefinite article, *an,* before vowel sounds: *an honest debate, an 1805 model.*

abbreviations

Be sparing in the use of abbreviations.

On first reference, spell out names of agencies, athletic conferences, firms, groups, organizations and school districts, except for abbreviations that are familiar to all readers, such as *P.T.A., U.S.* and *Y.M.C.A.* In subsequent references, use only those abbreviations that will be clear to readers. Do not follow a full name of a group or organization with an abbreviation in parentheses.

Do not use periods

1. for acronyms, initials that spell out pronounceable words: *NOW, UNESCO.*

2. when letters within a single word form an abbreviation: *TV.*

3. for *ACT, PSAT* and *SAT.*

4. for metric units: *cm, m, ml, kg,* etc.

See **academic degrees, addresses, period, standard forms, states and commonwealths.**

a cappella

academic degrees

Use abbreviations when they follow a name: *Jean Dubois, M.A.; Arthur Hernandez, Ph. D.; Mary Jones, Ed. D.*

Otherwise, write out: *He received his master's degree, and she received her doctorate.*

See **doctor.**

academic departments

Lowercase except for words that are proper nouns or adjectives: *science department, English department.*

accept, except

Accept means receive: *She accepts the candy.*

Except means exclude: *She accepted all the candy, except the licorice.*

accommodate

act, amendment, bill, law

Capitalize the full name or the name in general use: *Equal Rights Amendment* or *ERA.*

A measure is a bill until a legislature passes it and the chief executive signs it. Then it becomes a law.

action verb

Action verbs invigorate your writing; state-of-being verbs are static.

Use action verbs: *Jane conducts the choir.*

Avoid state-of-being verbs: *Jane is the choir's conductor.*

active voice, passive voice

The active voice shows who did what: *The principal changed the rule.*

The passive voice emphasizes what was done: *The rule was changed by the principal.*

It may obscure who did it: *The rule was changed.*

Stick to the active voice. Avoid the passive voice unless you have a reason: *The ball was hit for a home run—by a determined Roger Jones who has been playing baseball for 10 years with one arm.*

addresses

Abbreviate *Ave., Blvd., St.* and *Ter.* only in numbered addresses: *120 Columbus Ave., Columbus Avenue.*

Do not abbreviate *Circle, Drive, Lane, Place, Plaza, Point, Port, Oval* or *Road.*

Write out first through ninth when used as street names: *521 Fifth Ave.*

Abbreviate directions in numbered addresses: *23 N. 15th St.*

Write out direction if number is omitted: *North 15th Street.*

Abbreviate direction or area following names of streets: *345 Fifth St., N.W.*

See **abbreviations, directions and regions, numbers, states and commonwealths.**

advice, advise

Use *advice* as a noun: *I asked for advice.*

Use *advise* as a verb: *"I advise you to wait,"* she said.

adviser

To follow journalistic style, use *adviser.* Do not use *advisor.*

affect, effect

To *affect* means to influence: *The headline about the poll affected the voters.*

To *effect* means to bring about: *Through the referendum, voters effected a needed change.*

An *effect* is a result: *The new trade bill had a powerful effect on the auto industry.*

Avoid using *affect* as a noun except in the context of psychology, when it means a feeling: *His angry affect indicated that he felt his teacher's comment was unfair.*

affixes

Be consistent. Follow the dictionary the whole staff uses.

African-American
  See **hyphen, race.**

ageism
  Be direct in stating the age or age group. Use *16-year-old boy* or *71-year-old woman.*
  Avoid a patronizing tone. While *elderly* is acceptable in such phrases as *housing for the elderly,* do not refer to an individual as *elderly.* Do not use *elderly housing.*
  See **kid.**

ages
  Use numerals for ages: *He is 15, the 5-year-old boy, the 20-year-old.*
  Do not use an apostrophe with plurals: *She is in her 40s.*
  See **apostrophe.**

agreement
  Use singulars with singulars, plurals with plurals.
  Make pronouns and nouns match: *All the students want their pictures taken.*
  Not: *Everybody wants their picture taken.*
  Make subjects and verbs match: *Three members of the team are league all-stars. "Each member of the team is a winner," the coach said.*
  See **everybody, everyone; he/she, his/her; no one, nobody, none; pronouns.**

aggravate, irritate
  To *aggravate* is to make heavier, more serious, more severe: *When the timpani and the bass viols join the other instruments, they aggravate the mood.*
  To *irritate* is to annoy: *It will irritate the conductor if the bassoon comes in late.*

AIDS

Use this acronym on first reference for acquired immune deficiency syndrome.

a lot

Do not overuse this vague expression. If you ever do use it, be sure to spell it correctly as two words.

all

Hyphenate: *all-American, all-around, all-star.*

all ready, already

All ready means everyone is prepared: *Having reviewed the night before, we were all ready for the quiz.*

Already means previously: *I had already taken the quiz.*

all right

allege

Use with extreme caution. To *allege* means to assert without proof: *My teacher alleges that I haven't started my project.*

alma mater

An *alma mater* is a place from which someone has graduated: *As a member of the Class of 1997, his alma mater is Columbia College.*

alumna, alumnus/ alumnae, alumni

Use *alumna* to refer to an individual female graduate, *alumnus* to refer to an individual male graduate. Pluralize as *alumnae* for females and *alumni* for males. Refer to a mixed group as *alumni,* or use the English word: *graduates.*

See **graduate.**

a.m., p.m.
Write *2 p.m.*, not *2:00 p.m.* If the context is clear, just write *2*.
See **numbers.**

America
Because the term denotes the United States and all the other countries on the two continents in the Western Hemisphere, be more explicit. Except in directly quoted material, write *United States of America* or *U.S.A.* to denote the country. Write *U.S. citizen*, not *American citizen.*

among, between
Use *among* with more than two: *The five students divided the work among themselves.*
Use *between* with two: *They decided between two approaches to the assignment.*

ampersand {&}
Use this mark only when it is part of a school or company name. Do not use it merely to replace *and.*
See **company names, punctuation.**

Anglo
Avoid in referring to a non-Latin white.
See **Chicano, Hispanic, Latino, race.**

annual
Use to describe repetition for at least two years in a row.

ante
In general, do not hyphenate. *Ante* means before: *anteroom.*

anti

In general, do hyphenate. *Anti* means against: *anti-war.*

apostrophe {'}

Use an apostrophe

1. for singular and plural possessives: *The boy's story interested me. The girls' soccer team beat its opponent.*

2. for possessives ending in s: *two days' suspension, Doris' book.*

3. for joint possessives: *Bill and Ron's story.*

4. for contractions: *"Don't say it's over between us,"* *John pleaded.*

5. for omitted letters and numerals: *rock 'n' roll, '50s music, the Class of '99.*

6. to form the plural with letters of the alphabet: *He earned straight B's, the Oakland A's.*

Do not use an apostrophe

1. with possessive pronouns: *hers, its, yours.*

2. when a name without an apostrophe is official: *Newton Teachers Association.*

See **ages, possessive before gerund, punctuation.**

April Fools' Day

appositive

An appositive takes the place of another word or group of words in the same sentence: *My friend Jay* plays in the band. This sentence would make sense with just *my friend* or just *Jay,* which are in apposition to each other.

See **comma**.

Arabic names

Muslims all over the world use Arabic names. Follow an individual's preference.

Some Arabic names incorporate a definite article: *Anwar el-Sadat.* Others use three words: *Laila bint Humaid.*

The Arabic word for son—*ben, bin or ibn*—and daughter—*bint*—is sometimes part of a name: *Laila bint Humaid.* On second reference, in most instances, use only the last name in the series. *Abu*, meaning father of, should be retained: *Ahmed Abu Sabah, Abu Sabah.*

Geographical differences affect transliteration. Check individuals' preferred spellings.

See **names**.

army

Capitalize when referring to U.S. forces:
the *U.S. Army, the Army.* Otherwise, lowercase.

as you know

Unless you want to put readers on the defensive, do not use this expression.

Asian

Use *Asian(s)*, not *Asiatic(s)* and not *Oriental(s)*, when referring to people.

See **race.**

attribution

Cite sources for all statements a skeptical reader might question. Attributions should be as full and thorough as possible. They should appear early enough so that the reader can evaluate an assertion's validity and degree of bias.

Note: Unless two or more speakers are explicit about doing so, do not say they "agree" or "disagree" merely to effect a transition. Be meticulously accurate.

See **diction, editorializing, lead.**

average

Except in obviously informal uses, such as "I'm just an *average* kind of guy," specify *mean, median* or *mode.*

The *mean* is the sum divided by the number of addends. The *median* is the exact middle of a range: 10, 11, *16,* 23, 24. The *mode* is the number that occurs most often: 10, 11, *12, 12, 12,* 16.

See **percent, polls.**

a while

B

baby-sit, baby-sitting, baby sitter
Use with *for: I baby-sat for John.*
Not: *I baby-sat John.*

bar mitzvah, bas mitzvah, bat mitzvah
Use *bar mitzvah* for a boy. For a girl, use *bas mitzvah* or *bat mitzvah,* depending on her preference.

barbiturate

benefit, benefited, benefiting

berth, birth
Use as follows: *playoff berth, to give birth.*

Bible, bible
Capitalize and italicize for references to the Scriptures: *Bible.*
Lowercase for figurative uses: *The instruction manual became his bible while he built the model airplane.*

biological classification
Capitalize for genus, and lowercase for species: *Felis tigris.*

biweekly, semiweekly

Use *biweekly* to mean every two weeks. Use *semiweekly* to mean twice a week.

black

Use *black* rather than *Negro* except in proper names, such as *United Negro College Fund.*

See **race.**

boldface and italics

Use boldface and italics judiciously. Secure emphasis by a more forceful phrasing of the thought. This caution applies also to the use of entire words in uppercase or in boldface within a column of body type. Do not use boldface to point out titles in the context of a story.

Some publications, however, like to use one- or two-word all-cap or boldface lead-ins in longer articles to focus the reader's attention.

Note: Both boldface and italics are hard to read in large masses.

See **books, copy markings, debate subjects, headline, movies, plays, quotation marks, titles.**

bookkeeper

books

See **titles.**

boyfriend, girlfriend

brackets and parentheses

See **parentheses and brackets**.

brand names

Capitalize brand names. Use sparingly. Unless you

have a reason to specify a brand name, write *photo-copy*, not *Xerox*; *tissue*, not *Kleenex*.
   See **company names.**

burglary, larceny, robbery, theft
   In general, *burglars* enter a building with the inten-tion of committing a crime; they do not necessarily break in. *Larceny,* a legal term, means the wrongful taking of property. A non-legal, near synonym is *theft. Theft* is synonymous with stealing. *Robbery* involves the use of violence. This violence may be against per-sons or property. *Lockers are burglarized; people are robbed.*

bus, buses/bus, bused, busing
   Use for transportation.

buss, bussed, busses, bussing
   Use for kisses.

by
   In general, do not hyphenate: *bylaw.*

byline
   Use at the beginning of a story to give the name(s) of the author(s).

C

capitalization
   Use a minimum of capitalization.
   Capitalize
   1. proper nouns: *Cincinnati, Connecticut, the Debat-ing Club, the Nevada Athletic Association.*
   2. course titles, but not subject areas: *U.S. History, history.*
   3. a class with its year of graduation, but not names

of classes in the school: *the Class of 2004, the junior class, junior Bob Hennessey.*

4. full names of schools, but not *academy, college, high school* or *university* by themselves: *Brookline High School, the new high school.*

5. one-of-a-kind events and shortened forms of one-of-a-kind events: *Labor Day, the Series.*

6. languages: *English, Farsi, Italian, Mandarin.*

See **directions and regions, false titles, seasons, titles.**

Celsius

This measure of temperature used in the metric system sets its zero-degree point at the freezing point of water, or 32 degrees Fahrenheit. *Celsius* used to be called centigrade. To change to Fahrenheit, multiply by 9, divide by 5 and add 32.

center on

A center is a point. Write *center on.* Do not write *center around.*

chairman

Use *chairman* or *chair* for both sexes. Use *chairperson* only if it is the official title an organization uses.

Chicano

In general, prefer *Mexican-American.* Chicano may be used when activists apply it to themselves.

See **Anglo, Hispanic, Latino, race.**

Chinese names

Follow an individual's preference.

In China, the family name usually comes first with the given name second: Wang Li Wen.

Chinese people in other parts of the world may put

the given name first: *Jasmine Wang, Victor Wang.* If the given name is first, use the last name on second reference.

See **names**.

Christmas

Never use *Xmas.*

church

Capitalize as part of a formal name: *St. Andrew's Church, the Roman Catholic Church.*

city

Capitalize when part of a name: *Kansas City.* Lowercase for *city of Chicago.*

clauses and phrases

A clause has a subject and a verb, either stated or implied. All of the following are clauses: *I went to my locker...because I needed a sweater...Go see your editor.*

A dependent clause needs an independent clause to complete the thought: *When I lost my notes,* I had to redo the interview.

An independent clause may stand on its own as a sentence: *I had to redo the interview.*

A phrase lacks a subject and verb combination: *right on outdoors into the fresh air near the stadium...strawberry ripple with chocolate sauce, bananas and then some whipped cream and a cherry on top of that.*

See **comma, complex and compound sentences, semicolon.**

clichés

Don't use overworked expressions: *a dime a dozen, raining cats and dogs.*

co

Hyphenate words that denote occupation or status: *co-chairman, co-star.*

Do not hyphenate: *coeducation, cooperate, coordinate.*

coach

Do not capitalize.

coed

Use to denote education for males and females. Never use to mean a female student.

collective nouns

Use with singular verbs and singular pronouns: *The field hockey team is glad it met its goal.*

Use with plural pronouns when describing a group whose members act independently and individually: *The committee argued about the way the chairman counted their votes.*

See **agreement.**

colon {:}

Use a colon

1. before a quotation that begins a new paragraph.

2. before an independent clause that explains the beginning clause: *Pete can be too thorough: He left home this morning with four sets of keys—to the same car.*

3. before a series that forms an appositive: *Try this meal: soup, steak, salad, dessert and coffee.*

4. in scripts:

John: Marcia, don't leave me.

Marcia: Oh, John.

5. in Q and A:

Q: How will the school system find the money?

A: I don't know.

6. for time: *1:07.4.*

7. between the chapter and verse of a book in the *Bible*: *Job 3:16.*

Do not use a dash

1. with a colon.

2. before a list that follows a "to be" verb: *The athletes who received plaques are Susan Abrams, Bill Brown and Jennifer Chung.*

Do not overuse colons in headlines.

See **punctuation.**

comma {,}

Use a comma

•to separate

1. items in a series: *For lunch I had a tuna sandwich, chips, skim milk and chocolate ice cream.* Note that no comma is necessary to separate *skim milk* and *chocolate ice cream* because *and* already does so. Actually, each of the other commas replaces an understood *and.*

Sometimes, however, a comma is necessary before the *and*: *For lunch I had a tuna sandwich, chips, chocolate milk, and ice cream.* In this instance, if there were no comma before *and*, it might seem that both the milk and the ice cream were chocolate.

Or: *The players include sophomores Ed Andrews, Joe Russo and Tim Wilkins, and freshman Harry Schwartz.*

Here, the comma and second *and* show that Harry is part of a different group.

2. two modifiers, provided they are of the same kind and modify the noun, verb or adjective with equal force: *She gave him a cold, steady stare.*

Although the meanings of the words will usually indicate emphasis, one way to test whether the modifiers are equal is to reverse their order: *She gave him a steady, cold stare.*

Usually, meanings of words will indicate emphasis: *She has strong civic pride.*

3. elements in addresses: *Paul Gray, 999 Riverside Drive, New York, N.Y. 10025, is what it says on the mailing label.* Note that a comma is necessary after an address when the sentence continues.

4. groupings in numerals with more than three digits: *876,026,047.*

•to enclose parenthetical expressions:

5. nonessential clauses and phrases: *School journalists, who work hard, serve their schools.* The nonessential clause, which goes between commas, functions as almost a parenthetical, by-the-way expression. The reader infers that *all* school journalists work hard.

The essential adjectival clause, however, limits the meaning of the word it modifies. Without the commas, *only* the school journalists who work hard serve their schools: *School journalists who work hard serve their schools.*

6. nonessential appositives: *Tim Martinez, the track coach, expressed optimism.*

Some appositives, however, are essential to the meaning of a word or phrase and do not take a comma: *His friend Tim* specifies exactly which friend of all his friends.

Remember to put in the second comma after a parenthetical expression of several words: *The Cougars, North High School's team, won the meet.*

7. ages: *Harvey Webb, 17, will be a good photographer some day.*

8. a mild interjection: *Finally, alas, they broke up.*

9. nouns of address: *I ask you, Mr. Jones, why you disagree.*

10. dates: *I remember it was Wednesday, July 17, 1996, when he said so.* Note that a comma is neces-

sary after a date when the sentence continues.

11. yes, no: *Yes, I want to go.*

•to set off introductory material:

12. a phrase: *Smiling hungrily at the strawberry yogurt, he reached for his spoon.*

13. an adverb clause: *As he smiled hungrily at the strawberry yogurt, he reached for his spoon.*

14. attribution for a complete, directly quoted sentence: *The principal said, "I can't wait to read the yearbook."*

Note: Do not use a comma to set off a directly quoted word or phrase: *Barbara is the player who most consistently "puts team above self."*

15. a quotation or paraphrase followed by attribution: *"I can't wait to read the yearbook," the principal said.*

•before a coordinating conjunction followed by an independent clause

16. in compound sentences: *He moved to Texas, but her family stayed in Michigan.*

Use a comma before *and, but, for, nor, or* and *yet* when they link independent clauses.

But do not put a comma before *because: She won the human rights award because of her extensive volunteer work and passionate concern for justice.*

•in exceptional cases

17. for clarity: *To the sophomore, Harvey Webb was helpful. To the sophomore, Harvey, Webb was helpful.*

18. to indicate the omission of a verb in a compound sentence: *Jane was elected editor; May, assistant.*

See **addresses; appositives; attribution; clauses and phrases; complex and compound sentences; dates; punctuation; quotation marks; that, which.**

commitment

company names
Check for accurate spelling. Use Co. at the end. Do not use a comma before Inc. For example, write *Ajax Co. Inc.*

complex and compound sentences
A complex sentence has a dependent an independent clause: *While the girls' tennis team hosts South High, the boys' volleyball team hosts St. John's in sports action here this afternoon.*
A compound sentence has two or more independent clauses: *The girls' tennis team hosts South High, and the boys' volleyball team hosts St. John's in sports action here this afternoon.*
See **clauses and phrases.**

consistent

Constitution
Capitalize when referring to the *U.S. Constitution.* Capitalize the full name of a state constitution.

cooperate

coordinate

copy
This term denotes all material prepared for publication.

copy preparation
All copy must be neat and legible. Writers should submit stories on 8 $\frac{1}{2}$ by 11-inch white paper. Double- or triple-space, using one-inch margins. Use only one side of each sheet. Do not submit handwritten copy

unless absolutely necessary. For handwritten copy, use ink. Use lined paper and write on every other line. Print all proper names, technical terms and any other words that might be hard to decipher.

At the top left of the first sheet, put a word or phrase that identifies the topic and serves as a label. Under this label, put the number of words in the whole story and your name.

Start the story about one-third of the way down the first sheet.

Indent at least one inch for each new paragraph.

Note: If the story is to be poured from a disk, do not use tabs and do not hit the space key five times for each paragraph. Just use the ruler option. Later, when the story goes onto the page, indent no more than one em, the size of the uppercase M.

If the story continues beyond the first sheet, put MORE in the lower right. On the upper left of each successive sheet, put the page number, 2-2-2, 3-3-3, etc., and the label word. Circle the page number and label. Put MORE at the bottom right of each sheet except the last. Under the last line of the story, put 30, XXX or #.

Reread the story, checking for errors of fact, English usage, misspellings and other violations of style. Line out errors and write corrections over the line. Recount the words after you've made corrections.

Do not roll or fold the manuscript. Use a paper clip to hold the sheets together at the upper left.

See **em space.**

copyreader

Copyreaders should improve everything from content to style. They should check, correct and revise material carefully and neatly. The copy will be typeset, keyboarded or corrected exactly as received. If the copy is too full of markings, copyreaders should retype it.

Copyreaders should

1. check the word count after editing. The length must be accurate so as to correspond with the other elements in the page design. Don't send in too much or too little.

2. mark clear specifications on copy that is to appear in an unusual width. Column widths are measured in picas. Six picas equal one inch.

3. attach diagrams to show special arrangements. For example, if artwork is to be placed in a text wrap, attach a diagram showing the exact size of the space the artwork is to fill, together with its caption and credit.

4. mark in the margin of copy to specify unusual type faces, or larger or smaller type than is usual.

5. arrange copy, so far as possible, in the sequence in which it is to appear in print.

Note: Avoid the temptation to edit little by little as a story flows along on a computer screen. Read the story all the way through. Then edit it, preferably on a printout.

copyright

Obey copyright laws. Copyright means the exclusive right for the creator or owner of original artistic, literary or photographic material to make, distribute and control copies of that work for a specific number of years, as guaranteed by federal law. Copyright materials are available by writing the Registry of Copyright, Library of Congress, Washington, D.C. 20559.

See **attribution, "Plagiarism" essay, quotation**.

council, counsel, counselor

A *council* is a group that deliberates and discusses: *The Student Council met today.*

A *counsel* is advice: *He gave me thoughtful counsel.*

To *counsel* means to advise: *She counseled me to take chemistry.*

A *counselor* gives advice after consultation: *The guidance counselor helped me with my college planning.*

courtesy titles

Decide whether to use *Miss, Mr., Mrs.* or *Ms.*, and be consistent.

Most news publications do not use *Miss, Mr.* or *Mrs.* on first reference. Instead, they use the person's first name and last name: *principal Yvette Wilson.* In subsequent references, the writers use a consistent, shorter form: *Wilson.*

These publications may use courtesy titles in special contexts. To avoid ambiguity, for instance, *Mr.* and *Mrs.* would be used in references to a married couple or members of the same family: *John and Mary Smith* and then *Mr. Smith* or *Mrs. Smith.*

In a school where students address teachers as "Sir" or "Ma'am," the publication should use the person's courtesy title, first name and last name on first reference, and *Miss, Mr. , or Mrs.* with last name on subsequent references.

Avoid referring to a woman as *Mrs. John Smith.* Write her first name: *Mrs. Mary Smith.*

Do not use *Ms.* unless a source requests it.

See **cutline, false titles, identifications, names, titles.**

curriculum, curricula

Curriculum is singular; *curricula* is plural.

cutline

Give each piece of artwork its own cutline, also called a caption. Use a standard phrasing and typographical form to credit all photos and illustrations.

Wait until the picture is in front of you. Study it. Crop it. Then write the cutline.

Begin with concrete words to describe the persons, action and scene of a photo or illustration. Include full names and identifications of all who are clearly visible, including members of opposing teams in sports photos.

For group photos in yearbooks, begin the cutline with the name of the group in a contrasting type. Then label by rows, front to back.

Cutlines for photos that run without related stories should be full sentences that give the who, what, when, where, why and how.

For photos and drawings that accompany stories, include in the cutline sentence(s) the information that connects the art to the story.

Use present tense to describe the action in the picture. Then switch to the past tense and add the information that completes the action: *Principal Mark Simon greets freshmen James Olsen and Ellen MacDougall as they enter the building. The Class of 2000 participated in orientation Thursday, Sept. 5. Upperclassmen arrived Friday, Sept. 6, and classes began.*

See **courtesy titles, false titles, identifications, titles.**

D

dangling modifiers

Modifiers must refer clearly to some other word in a sentence.

A sentence containing a dangling modifier doesn't make sense: *After running onto the field, the game began.* The sentence should say, *After running onto the field, the teams began the game.*

See **misplaced modifier**.

dash {—}

Dashes are usually separators. A dash is twice the length of a hyphen.

Use dashes

1. to show an abrupt change in emphasis, action or

thought: *He said, "Bring me that"— but he was gone.*

2. to indicate faltering or broken speech: *"Well— er— you see— it was this way."*

3. to denote an unexpected change in sentiment: *He was generous—with other people's money.*

4. after datelines: *MUNCIE, Ind.—.*

5. before a name at the end of material, such as a letter to the editor or a long quotation, as in—*Charles Nash, freshman.*

Be sparing with dashes.

See **hyphen, punctuation.**

data

Use a plural verb for several kinds of individual items: *These data show the need for higher taxes.*

Use a singular verb for *data* as a unit: *This data is accurate.*

dates

Keep the date of publication in mind when writing for newspaper readers. *Today* is the date of publication; *tomorrow,* the day after publication; *yesterday,* the day before publication. Do not use future tense for events that should be past tense on the publication date.

Write *Saturday, March 15,* specifying the name of the day and month, and date in numerals unless references fall within one week of publication. In that case use *today, tomorrow, yesterday* or *the day of the week (Saturday).*

Do not use *on* before a date.

Do not write *March 15th.*

Never use *st, nd, rd, th* after a numeral in a date.

See **months.**

days of the week

Do capitalize; do not abbreviate: *Monday, Tuesday. . .*

de
In general, no hyphen: *demobilize.*

debate subjects
Punctuate and capitalize as follows: *The subject for debate was "Resolved: That capital punishment should be abolished in the United States."*
See **boldface and italics, quotation marks.**

defamation
Defamatory material hurts someone's reputation.
See **libel, slander.**

definitely

diction
This term denotes the words a writer chooses. In making decisions about words to use, consider connotation and context. Keep the tone of the publication forthright and fair.
Do not jar your reader. Avoid becoming suddenly slangy or colloquial in a piece of serious news reporting or opinion. Save such devices for special features or humor columns.
See **attribution, editorializing.**

dimensions
Use numerals. Write out *inches, feet, yards,* etc.: *She is 5 feet 7 inches tall.*

different from
Use *different from: The teachers' statement is different from the school board's.*
Avoid *different than.*

directions and regions
Lowercase directions: *She drove west on the free-*

way.

Capitalize regions: *That's what I like about the South.*

Do not capitalize *north, south, east, west* and their compounds and derivatives except when they designate sections of the country or form proper names or well-known sections of a city: *the West Coast, the South End, the Lower East Side.*

See **addresses, capitalization.**

disabled

People with disabilities may prefer particular terminology for descriptions. Check with the person. Avoid stereotyping.

disc jockey

diseases

Lowercase unless a disease includes a proper name: *diabetes, leukemia, Alzheimer's disease, Gehrig's disease.*

dispel, dispelled, dispelling

doctor

Use *Dr.* in a first reference to a person who holds an M.D., a doctor of medicine degree. *Dr.* may also be used in a first reference to a person who holds a Ph. D. (doctor of philosophy) or Ed. D. (doctor of education).

See **academic degrees.**

dollars and cents

Use the $ and numerals except in amounts of more than six figures: *The equipment is valued at $418,000. The project cost $1.2 million.*

Do not write *$.50, 50 cts.* or *$0.50.* Write *50 cents.*

See **numbers.**

doughnut

downtown

dyslexia

E

each other

editor in chief

editorial
   This persuasive, polished piece of writing represents the position of the publication as a whole. It is unsigned and uninitialed, in contrast to a column, which is bylined.

editorializing
   Editorializing is using unattributed opinions or adverbs or adjectives that color the facts, resulting in explicit or implicit bias.
   While completely objective reporting is impossible, you should avoid editorializing except in material clearly labeled opinion.
   Editorializing must not appear in straight news stories. Such words as *interesting, important, claims* and *feels* indicate that the writer is drawing conclusions, not giving straight facts.
   Imperatives and exhortations have no place in straight reporting. Thus, sentences such as *"Go, Tigers!"* or *"All students should show their school spirit tonight in the gym"* should never appear unless they are attributed to a specific source.
   See **attribution, diction, headline, lead.**

elections
   Use the following punctuation and capitalization: *The*

new officers are Georgia Lower, president; William Morrison, vice president; Charles Ewart, secretary; James Pendleton, treasurer.

Alternate order: *The new officers are president, Georgia Lower; vice president, William Morrison; secretary, Charles Ewart; treasurer, James Pendleton.*

See **semicolon.**

ellipsis {. . .}

Three periods separated by spaces show that words have been omitted from a quotation: *"This generation . . . will see a revival of learning."*

At the end of a sentence, use a fourth period.

See **punctuation, quotation marks.**

em space

Many news publications use the *em space*, which is the size of an M, at the start of each paragraph.

See **copy preparation**.

employee(s)

en route

everybody, everyone

Use with singular pronouns and verbs: *Everybody wants his own way. She asked everyone to be a good sport.*

But: *Every one of the vandals was suspended.*

See **no one, nobody, none.**

ex

Use a hyphen when this prefix denotes former: *George Hansen, an ex-quarterback.*

ex officio

exaggerate

excel, excelled, excelling

exclamation point {!}
   Prefer the period. Use exclamation points to show only unusually strong emotion: *"Help! Help!" he yelled as a swarm of bees chased him across the field.*
   See **punctuation.**

extracurricular

eyewitness

F

fairgrounds

false titles
   False titles describe a person's occupation or area of skill without specifying exact professional authority: *politician, soprano soloist, J.V. defensive tackle.*
   Some pointers:
   1. Do not use false titles adjectivally before a person's name as in *rookie goal tender Jean Farlow.* Instead, set the name off from the descriptive phrase with commas: *Jean Farlow, a rookie goal tender, excelled during the game.*
   2. Never capitalize false titles.
   3. Sometimes it is desirable to avoid overuse of commas, as with *sophomore Mark Jones, English teacher Brenda Foster* or *soccer coach John Meyer.* But with these one- or two-word expressions from the school press as exceptions, the appositive is usually best: *Sally Harris, a violist, plays in the orchestra.*
   4. Base decisions about the use of the definite or indefinite article on whether the individual is well known:

Jim Chang, the actor, spoke on careers in theater. Barbara Barnes, a member of the club, served refreshments.

See **comma, courtesy titles, identifications, political titles, religious titles, titles.**

farewell

farther, further
Use *farther* to refer to distance: *He ran two miles farther up the road than John did.*

Use *further* to refer to degree: *He saw further consequences of the staff cuts.*

fewer, less
Use *fewer* when referring to separate items: *I am applying to fewer colleges than he is.*

Use *less* when referring to a quantity or a total: *She has less than $100 left.*

finalize
Do not use. Instead, write *finish* or *complete.*
See **jargon.**

First Amendment
The Constitution's First Amendment forbids Congress from making any law that abridges the freedom of speech or of the press. In a series of cases, the U.S. Supreme Court has interpreted the Fourteenth Amendment of the Constitution to extend this prohibition to states and their agents, which include public schools and colleges. The First Amendment does not provide these rights to the student press at private or sectarian schools and colleges.

In a 1969 decision, the Court created specific interpretations of First Amendment rights for public school and college student publications. *Tinker v. Des Moines*

Independent Community School District involved symbolic speech. After school officials had warned them not to, three students wore black armbands to school in 1965 to protest the Vietnam War. When the students were suspended, their parents took the case to court. The Court held that prohibiting the wearing of armbands could not be sustained unless it "materially and substantially interferes with the operation of the school."

The Court's *Hazelwood* decision of 1988, however, says public school administrators may use broad powers to control school-sponsored student expression.

After *Hazelwood*, Massachusetts, Iowa, Colorado, Kansas and Arkansas reaffirmed public school students' rights to determine the content of school-sponsored publications. California already had a law that dates from 1977 protecting students' free expression.

See **forum, forum theory**.

fiscal year
This term denotes a 12-month period that a governmental body, such as a school system, uses for bookkeeping purposes. A fiscal year might not coincide with the calendar year.

follow up, follow-up
Use without a hyphen for a verb: *She asked him to follow up the story.*

Use with a hyphen for an adjective: *He wrote the follow-up story.*

foresight

forum
The term denotes a medium through which people express a variety of views.

forum theory

This term refers to the legal concept that in a public high school or public college, when the publication provides a forum for student opinion, and where taxpayers provide the funding for the publication, no one person stands in the position of publisher and the state has an obligation to maintain the publication as a forum.

Under *Hazelwood,* a public high school publication may be reaffirmed or established as a public forum if school administrators decide to do so.

See **First Amendment, publisher**.

Four-H

Write *4-H Club,* and *4-H'ers* for members.

fractions

Write out and hyphenate fractions if they are less than one: *one-fifth, two-thirds.*

See **numbers.**

french fries

freshman, freshmen

Use *freshman* as a singular noun: *Ed O'Connor, a freshman.*

Use *freshman* as an adjective: *freshman year, freshman soccer team.*

Use *freshmen* as a plural noun: *The freshmen elected Mary Ross president.*

full time, full-time

Do not hyphenate as an adverb: *He teaches full time.*

Do hyphenate as an adjective: *He is a full-time teacher.*

G

gay
   Use as an adjective: *the gay and lesbian activists.*
   Do not use as a noun to mean homosexual unless the word appears in a quotation or as part of the name of an organization.
   Do not use such expressions as *"He is a gay"* or *"That's gay."*

girl, boy/woman, man
   Use *girl* or *boy* until the age of 18. Then use *woman* or *man*: *She had lunch with the girl on the varsity gymnastics team. The boy decided to go out for track.*
   Do not use women's or men's to apply to teams or programs at the high school level: *girls' basketball, boys' swimming.*
   See **lady**.

good, well
   Use *good* as an adjective: *She is a good director.*
   Use *well* as an adverb: *The show is going well.*

goodbye

government

grade
   Hyphenate compounds and use numerals: *9th-grader, a 12th-grade student.*
   See **hyphen.**

graduate
   Always use *graduate* with *from* as a verb: *He will graduate from high school.*

Not: *"He graduated high school."*
See **alumna, alumnus/alumnae, alumni.**

graf
Instead of full paragraphs, news publication writers use grafs. These one- or two-sentence units pick up the reading pace through the additional white space that results from frequent indentions.
See **paragraphs.**

grown-up

gubernatorial

H

halfback

Hanukkah

headline
Summarize and emphasize the stories' content in headlines. They should say enough to attract and inform readers, but no more. Headlines should fit their allotted spaces.

Each item set in body type—news stories, editorials, letters to the editor, briefs—should carry a headline of its own, not merely a label.

Most newspaper headlines imply complete sentences. Some guidelines:

1. Study the lead and the rest of the story.

2. If the story has a summary lead, state its gist in a sentence.

3. Try to put the key word first.

4. Do not editorialize, except over an opinion piece.

Use subjects and verbs to make a complete statement of fact.

5. Use short words in a headline. The more you tell, the better; seldom will just two or three words suffice.

6. Use action verbs rather than state-of-being verbs.

7. Avoid *a, an, the* and *and.*

8. Use present tense for action that has occurred: *Department head resigns.*

9. Use the conditional tense or infinitive for action that is about to occur: *Teacher might apply for department head job; Principal to retire.*

10. Try to use the active voice.

11. Place the subject and verb in the first line if possible.

12. Never divide words in headlines. From the top line to the next, do not separate parts of an infinitive, a noun and its modifiers or article, a preposition and its object, a conjunction from the words it joins, or a participle from its auxiliary.

13. Use a minimum of capitalization. Most newspapers use downstyle. In downstyle, capitalization occurs as it would in a sentence. The first letter of the first word is capitalized as are the first letters of proper nouns: *Chorus sings, sightsees in Chicago.*

In upstyle, the first letter of the first word and of all other words except articles, conjunctions, and prepositions of three or fewer letters are capitalized: *Chorus Sings, Sightsees in Chicago.*

Whichever style you use, be consistent.

14. Punctuate when necessary only. Use the period for abbreviations only. Use single quotation marks: *Mayor cites 'terrific' team*

15. Numbers may be in figures or written out regardless of copy rule. It is permissible to begin a headline with numerals. When a numeral is longer than its corresponding word, use the word: *200 million,* not *200,000,000.*

16. Do not repeat the thought in the second deck that you stated in the first.

17. Write a feature headline for a feature story.

See **active voice, passive voice; action verb; capitalization; editorializing; kicker; lead; numbers; punctuation; subhead.**

he/she, his/her

Do not use these pronouns with slashes. Change to *they* or *their*, making certain to change attending verbs and referents appropriately.

Use matching plurals: *Although students may want to take their time walking down the hall, they should get to class promptly.*

Avoid the cumbersome slashed singular: *Although a student may want to take his/her time walking down the hall, he/she should get to class promptly.*

See **agreement, pronouns.**

Hispanic

Avoid except in reference to people of Spanish or Portuguese descent.

See **Anglo, Chicano, Latino, race.**

hold

This word is easily overworked. One editor says a person can *hold* a package or a baby, but not a meeting, a dance, a party or an election.

Be concise: *meet.* Try different verbs: *host a dance, give a party, run an election.*

homeroom

hopefully

Hopefully is an adverb that means in a hopeful manner: *The child looked hopefully at the cookie jar.*

Do not use *hopefully* to mean *I hope* or *Let's hope*, as in *Hopefully, it will be sunny tomorrow.*

hyphen {-}
Use a hyphen
1. to indicate the joining of two or more words to express one idea: *secretary-treasurer, president-elect.*
2. to indicate two heritages: *Italo-American, Japanese-American.*
3. in compound modifiers: *up-to-date style, game-winning homer.*
4. with compound numbers: *seventy-five.*
5. to avoid confusion and ambiguity: *two year-old boys, 2-year-old boys.*
6. in suspensive constructions: *the 14-, 15- and 16-year-olds.*
7. to label an academic year: *In the 1998-99 school year, he took French for the first time.*
Use prepositions, not hyphens, in formal writing with *from. . . to*: *She attended this school from 1996 to 2000.*
Do not use a hyphen in civil or military titles: *attorney general, brigadier general.*
See **punctuation, syllabication.**

I

"i" before "e"
As the old rule goes, make it "i" before "e" except after "c" or when sounded as "ay" as in *neighbor* or *weigh.*
But: *Neither leisured foreign sovereign seized the heifer on the weird heights.*

identifications
Identify people in stories and cutlines.
Some principles:
1. Use their first and last names and titles.

2. Choose the most pertinent identification for the first reference: *senior Ellen Chan; Ellen Chan, the first singles player; Ellen Chan, a tennis co-captain.*

3. Somewhere in a story, include students' classes and teachers' departments.

4. Never overload identifications: *senior co-captain first singles player Ellen Chan.*

See **attribution, courtesy titles, cutline, false titles, names, religious titles, titles.**

ideologies

Lowercase them when they denote political philosophies: *He is a conservative, and she is a liberal.*

Capitalize them when they refer to political parties or when they are derived from a proper name: *Conservatives, Liberal Democrats, Marxists, Nazis.*

See **political parties.**

illustrations

Choose art that will reproduce clearly.

In line art, the strokes must be sharp and clear. The image will appear with no gradations of gray.

In a halftone, the individual element is the dot. Collectively, halftone dots represent the image of a continuous tone original. In proportion as the dots are large and close together or small and far apart, the tones in the printed picture will vary from black to white. Halftones are classified according to the degree of fineness or coarseness of the screen used on the copy camera. Meshes vary from 60 to 400 lines to the inch. The finer screens bring out the detail and artistic quality of a picture. The type of paper used will more or less determine the screen.

When using a computer to place and process illustrations, make sure that however the image gets into the computer, the quality of the output compares fa-

vorably to what is visible on the screen.
See **cutline.**

impact
Use as a noun: *The impact of the punch knocked him out.*
Do not use as a verb: *This level of funding should impact the program.*
See **jargon**.

impel, impelled, impelling

important
Do not write *importantly.*

in
In general, no hyphen: *incomparable.*

inasmuch as

incur, incurred, incurring

indispensable

informational graphics
The maps, charts, graphs and diagrams that include illustrations and/or photography should be neat, concise and accurate. Visual messages should conform to the facts. Credit the source of a graphic or part of a graphic.
See **average, cutline, percent, polls.**

intramural, interscholastic
Intramural means within one school: *Floor hockey is an intramural sport at this school.*
Interscholastic means between or among schools: *The*

athletic director helped to set up an interscholastic schedule among five schools.

italics

See **boldface and italics.**

its, it's

Its is possessive: *The dog wagged its tail.*
It's is the contraction for *it is*: *It's raining.*
See **apostrophe.**

J

jargon

Use plain English: *She set deadlines. We discussed what we hoped students would learn.*

Don't use jargon, the inflated language that sounds important and in-groupy but means little: *She utilized parameters for input. We held discussions around learning outcomes.*

Avoid overuse of the suffix *-wise* as in, *Weatherwise, it will probably hail.*

job titles

Use *firefighter, journalist, police officer.*
Not: *fireman, newsman, policeman.*

Jr., Sr.

Do not put a comma between the name and *Jr.* or *Sr.:*
Paul Farrell Jr.
See **capitalization.**

judgment

junior, senior

Never abbreviate classes: *junior class, senior class.*

K

ketchup

kicker

This design device attracts attention. In headlines, kickers are small-sized type above the main headline. Wording of the kicker should differ from the wording of the main headline.

In cutlines, the first word or short phrase may be set off in display type. These few words function as mini headlines for cutlines. Kickers work well with photographs that stand alone.

See **cutline, headline, subhead.**

kid

Use kid to denote a baby goat, not as a synonym for child or student unless the context calls for informality. See **ageism.**

kilogram

A term for 1,000 grams, this measurement of weight is part of the metric system. To convert to pounds, multiply by 2.2.

kilometer

A kilometer is 1,000 meters, or about 3,281 feet or five-eighths of a mile. To convert to miles, multiply by 0.62.

kindergarten

know-how

knowledgeable

kosher

L

lady

Just as *gentleman* is not a synonym for *man, lady* is not a synonym for *woman.* Some girls and women find the use of lady, as in *The Lady Tigers won the meet,* demeaning.

See **girl, boy/ woman, man.**

Latino

This term refers to all people of Latin American descent. It's best to be specific: *Brazilian, Colombian.*

See **Anglo, Chicano, Hispanic, race.**

lead

Establish the tone, focus and direction for a story in a concise opening paragraph called a lead.

In the lead, set up a structure that will best show how and why whatever has happened or is about to happen is likely to affect readers.

Reporters should ask themselves: If I were telling the story in ordinary conversation, what single fact would I tell first? In most instances, who did it, what happened or may happen, why it happened or how it happened would be stressed over when and where it happened.

One way to begin a story about breaking news is with a lead that summarizes the most important facts in the story and presents these news elements in order of descending importance. These elements are embodied in the five W's—who, what, when, where, why—and one H—how. Good summary leads include only the most important W's and H in a declarative sentence.

But just as a summary lead would be inappropriate for a story that needs to build to a punch line, beginning at the beginning is certainly a poor choice for breaking news or sports.

For less timely features and for editorials, writers have much more flexibility. One option is to begin at the beginning and develop a chronological narrative. Others are to start with a problem the rest of the story explains or solves, or to begin with an interesting image, or with a short, revealing incident.

After the opening section, the feature or editorial writer might make use of a summary statement, a thesis statement or a thematic sentence as a bridge to the rest of the story.

Further pointers:

1. Be accurate.

2. Be fair.

3. Attribute in the lead anything that is not generally known.

4. Do not use cumbersome labels within leads. Avoid such constructions as *The Central High School girls' varsity lacrosse team...*

5. Include only the most important of the W's and H. Try to decide whether a W or H would add significantly to a reader's understanding.

6. When using a summary lead, follow the order of the elements in the lead in presenting the rest of the story.

7. Avoid overuse of the school name. The reader can assume it happened in school unless notified.

8. Set a strict limit on the number of leads in an issue that begin with questions or direct quotations.

9. Make the opening words concrete. Avoid *it is, there is, a, an, the.*

10. Use the active voice.

11. Use action verbs, not state-of-being verbs, keeping in mind that news usually concerns change.

12. Use third person, except for words in direct quotations. Avoid *you.* Reserve *our, we* and *us* for editorials. Seldom use *I.*

13. Unless a name is widely known, delay its use until the second or third graf. This practice is called using a blind lead:

Three sophomores will compete in a speech tournament next week.

The second graf would say:

Jane Abrams, Harold Cutler and Barbara Walsh will travel to Springfield for . . .

14. Do not begin with a dictionary definition: *Webster's defines sportsmanship as . . .*

15. Remember that most headlines are based on the information in the lead. Headlines tend to emphasize who and what, rather than when and where.

Leads, like headlines, take a lot of practice.

See **active voice, passive voice; action verb; attribution; dates, editorializing; headline.**

learning disability

Use this term with care. Consult people in school for appropriate, up-to-date terms. Never use *L.D.* as a label.

left-handed

letters to the editor

If space permits, publish guidelines for letter writers. The staff can reserve the right to edit letters.

Use a standard form for openings and signatures. Give each letter its own headline.

liaison

libel

Only a court can determine if a statement is libelous. In general, the term refers to defamation that is published and is not provably true.

See **defamation, slander.**

like and as

Like is a preposition: *My tears fell like rain.*

As is a subordinating conjunction: *As I said to my teacher that I had decided to switch out of the class, I knew I was making the right move.*

Never use *like* to mean *said*: *I'm like, "Why shouldn't I?"*

And she's like, "Well, that's just sooo totally cheesy."

lists

In stories, alphabetize lists of names or items of equal rank.

livable

M

manageable

many, most

Avoid vague terms. Whenever possible, use exact amounts. If you do not know the exact amounts, do some research. Be sure to attribute the information to sources.

See **attribution.**

media

Medium is singular: *The school newspaper is a medium.*

In general, use *media* with a plural verb: *The media often distort news about problems in high schools.*

medieval

meter

A meter equals 39.37 inches. To convert meters to inches, multiply by 39.37. To convert meters to yards, multiply by 1.1.

middle age, middle-aged

million, billion
Use with numerals: *1.7 million, $3 billion.*
See **numbers.**

misplaced modifier
Put a modifier next to the word it modifies. A misplaced modifier destroys your logic: *Joan Clark looked for an antique bed for her mother with an inlaid marble head.* The sentence should say: *Joan Clark looked for an antique bed with an inlaid marble head for her mother.*
See **dangling modifier**.

Miss, Mr., Mrs., Ms.
See **courtesy titles.**

misspell

months
Capitalize names of months. Abbreviate, except months with six letters or fewer, when used with a date: *Thursday, Jan. 15; Friday, July 10.*
See **comma, dates.**

movies
See **titles.**

mph
Use without periods.

N

names
Follow these guidelines:
1. Use full names on first reference.

2. Always verify spelling. Is it *Coan? Coen? Cohan? Cohen? Kohn?*

3. Unless a person prefers a nickname, use the given name.

4. Do not abbreviate given names, as in *Alex., Chas., Geo., Thos., Wm.*

See **Arabic names, Chinese names.**

nearsighted

newcomer

newsstand

no one, nobody, none

These words usually mean no single one. They take singular pronouns and verbs: *No one wants his locker next to hers. Nobody in his right mind misses a detention. None of these cuts is really an absence.*

Do not use *their, they* or *them* with *no one, nobody* and *none.*

Never write: *No one wants their locker next to hers. Nobody in their right mind misses a detention. None of these cuts are really an absence.*

See **agreement; everybody, everyone.**

noon

Do not write *12 o'clock noon* or *12 noon.* Just write *noon.*

nowadays

numbers

Write out *one* through *nine* and *first* through *ninth.* Use numerals for 10 and above.

When numbers include decimals, use *and.* For those

without decimals, do not use *and*: *Three dollars and five cents is my total profit. Two hundred three dollars will pay for all those books.*

Do not begin a sentence with a numeral. Instead, write it out or rephrase the thought. Years are the only exception: *2003 is the year when they will graduate.*

More samples of usage:

1. *Last year 1,950 students enrolled, bringing the student-teacher ratio to 16-to-1.*

2. *More than a hundred people tried out.*

3. *Walker dropped one over from the 30-yard mark.* (Note the hyphen.)

4. *She is the No. 2 singles player.*

5. *His time was 10.2 seconds.*

6. *The image occurs in Act II, scene ii, line 2.*

7. *Mix 1 tablespoon of sugar with 2 teaspoons of grated orange peel. Add 2 eggs.*

See **addresses; a.m., p.m.; averages; dates; dollars and cents; fractions; percent; scores; standard forms, titles, weights.**

O

occur, occurred, occurring

only

Use with care to avoid editorializing as in, *The ice cream cost only $2.50,* or *The principal made only two main points in his address to the faculty.*

See **editorializing.**

optimist

oral, verbal

Use *oral* for spoken words: *She gave an oral report.*

Use *verbal* to mean any kind of communication with words: *The verbal message is clearer than the visual.*

over, more than

Use *over* with heights: *He jumped over the fence.*

Use *more than* with quantities: *More than 1,000 watched the game.*

overall

P

paragraphs

Newspaper paragraphs should be no longer than eight printed lines, or 35 to 50 words. Vary the words that begin successive paragraphs unless your repetition is deliberate.

See **graf.**

parallel structure

Use parallel structure to keep your writing brisk and balanced: *He likes apples, oranges and pears. . . red apples, juicy oranges and ripe pears. . . bright red apples, sweet juicy oranges and fresh ripe pears.*

Not: *He likes apples, juicy oranges and fresh ripe pears.*

parentheses {( )} and brackets {[ ]}

Avoid overuse of parentheses and brackets.

Use parentheses

1. for nicknames after given names: *William (Chip) Logan.*

2. for interpolations: *The Berlin (N.H.) group visited Paris (Maine).*

Put the period outside the parentheses if the material inside is not a full sentence: *Marcie Ryan scores a point (photo by Virginia Mason).*

Although it is usually smoother to paraphrase, brackets can show that the writer has added material to a direct quotation: *"I spoke to Irwin [superintendent Gre-*

gory Irwin]."
   See **abbreviations, punctuation, quotation marks.**

peninsula

percent
   Write it out. Give the base, which is the figure from which the percentage is derived: *Twenty percent of the 10 students failed.*
   See **average, polls.**

period {.}
   Use a period
   1. at the end of every declarative sentence.
   2. after most abbreviations: *The Goss Co., the Rev. Joseph Higgins, Rep. Barney Frank, 104 West St.*
   3. as a decimal point: *Your score on the test is 86.5.*
   Do not use a period
   1. after chemical symbols: *CuO (copper oxide).*
   2. after radio call letters or in network abbreviations: *KNBC, CBS.*
   See **abbreviations, ellipsis, punctuation.**

permissible

personal, personnel
   Personal means an individual's own ideas or concerns: *This letter is private and personal.*
   Personnel means a group of employees or an administrative division that focuses on persons a company or other institution employs: *There was material in his file in the personnel office.*

plagiarism
   Plagiarism means passing off someone else's work as your own.

Avoid even the suspicion of plagiarism. Give credit to all sources you have used including CD-ROMs and the Internet.

See **copyright, "Plagiarism" essay, quotation.**

plays
See **titles.**

political parties
Capitalize the *Democratic Party,* the *Republican Party.* Capitalize *Communist, Conservative, Liberal, Socialist,* etc., when they refer to political parties. Lower case when they denote a political point of view: She is a *liberal Republican.*
See **ideologies.**

political titles
Be consistent.
Some samples of usage:
1. *Rep. Mary Garcia spoke with Gov. Ed Quinn, Sen. William Jones and Mayor Margaret Lincoln.*
2. *State Reps. John Doe, D-Des Moines, and Jane Doe, R-Perry, sponsored the bill.*
See **false titles, identification, names, titles.**

polls
In writing about polls, summarize the results. Tell how many people were polled and the range, nature and size of the sample. Tell who took the poll and when, how and where the person(s) took it. Whenever possible, provide the probable error, such as +/- 3 percent.
See **average, percent.**

possessive before gerund
Use the possessive form of a noun or pronoun before

a gerund (verb form used as a noun): *Sam's losing his match cost the team a victory. Mom was thrilled at my winning the piano competition.*

See **apostrophe**.

postgraduate

predominant, predominate

Predominant, an adjective, means having superior strength: *The painter used red as the predominant color.*

To *predominate* means to exert control: *In the painting, red predominated.*

principal, principle

As an adjective, *principal* means main: *Blue is the principal color.*

As a noun, *principal* means the main one: *The principal announced a new schedule.*

A *principle* is a moral or theoretical tenet: *Freedom of expression is an important principle.*

privilege, privileged

pronouns

Make pronoun references accurate and clear.

Some guidelines:

1. Make pronouns agree with their antecedents: *The team beat its opponent.*

Not: *The team beat their opponent.*

2. Be accurate with cases. Use the nominative case, not the objective case, for a subject: *He is older than I am. My friends and I like to go out for lunch. He and I are lab partners.*

Not: *He is older than me. Me and my friends like to go out for lunch. Him and me are lab partners.*

Use the objective case, not the nominative case, for an object: *It was a secret between him and me.*

Not: *It was a secret between him and I.*

2. Use *he* or *his* when the antecedent is masculine or common: *Nobody in his right mind would want to study today.*

3. Use *she* and *her* to refer to feminine nouns: *The Queen Elizabeth 2 left her berth.*

4. If a pronoun reference is unclear, drop the pronoun and use the noun: *Buffalo is my hometown* is clearer than *It is my hometown.*

See **agreement; he/she, his/her.**

publisher

In the commercial or private school press, this term denotes the owner of a publication. In public high schools, depending on state laws and local policies, this term may refer to the local school board.

See **First Amendment.**

punctuation

Punctuate for clarity only. Avoid unnecessary punctuation.

See **ampersand, apostrophe, colon, comma, dash, ellipsis, exclamation point, hyphen, parentheses and brackets, period, question mark, quotation marks, semicolon.**

Q

quarterback

question mark {?}

Use at the end of a direct question: *Did you say, "I hate field trips"? We asked, "Will he go?" "Should I stay?" he asked.*

Do not use at the end of an indirect question: *He asked if he should stay.*

See **punctuation, quotation marks.**

quotation

Be accurate when quoting, and be sure to specify the source of every quotation. Keep speakers' words in context. If words were said in a joking manner, you should usually say so.

Use quotations from your sources to support and illustrate your story, choosing newsworthy remarks that express people's individuality: *"It's a realistic challenge to present 'Richard II' with a high school cast,"* the director said.

Otherwise, paraphrase. Never pad as in, *"The curtain goes up at 7:30 Thursday evening, and tickets will cost $7.50 at the door,"* the director said.

See **attribution, copyright, ellipsis, parentheses and brackets, "Plagiarism" essay, stacked quotations.**

quotation marks {" "} and {' '}

Place commas and periods inside quotation marks: *He said, "I never know what lunch we take in this class."* If other punctuation is part of the quoted material, place it inside the quotation marks: *He asked, "Do we take first lunch?"* If not, place the punctuation outside: *Why do you keep saying, "I know we have second lunch"?*

Use quotation marks

1. to indicate that the words are those of another person: *"He is alive!" the boy shouted. The coach called the team "just great—a terrific group."*

Note: Neither a comma nor a capital is necessary when quoting a short piece of a sentence.

2. at the beginning of each paragraph in a quotation of several paragraphs, and at the end of the last paragraph of the series.

3. to express irony: *The "game" turned into a brawl.*

4. to introduce unfamiliar words: *The "dingbat" is a typographical device.*

5. Use single quotation marks to set off quotations

within quotations: *"When he told me, 'You won the prize,' it was just incredible,"* the actor said.

Do not use quotation marks

1. around a paraphrase.

2. around nicknames.

3. in copy made up largely of titles.

4. with names of newspapers and other periodicals

5. with *Bible,* or such reference materials as *encyclopedias* .

See **attribution, boldface and italics, cutline, ellipsis, headline, parentheses and brackets, punctuation, titles.**

quotes, quotations

Use *quotes* as a verb: *She often quotes Maya Angelou.*

Use *quotations* as a noun: *He likes to write quotations from Bill Clinton on the blackboard.*

R

race

Mention a person's race, nationality, ethnic group or religion only when required for the reader to make sense of what you have written.

See **African-American, America, Anglo, Asian, black, Chicano, Hispanic, hyphen, Latino.**

redundancy

Be concise: *He nominated her.*

Not: *He placed her name in nomination.*

Eliminate repeated words: *She lives in Richmond, Va.*

Not: *She lives in the city of Richmond in the commonwealth of Virginia.*

Delete adjectives and adverbs that restate what nouns and verbs imply: *She ran up the stairs. She had brought her week-old baby to school.*

Not: *She ran quickly up the stairs. She had brought her little week-old baby to school.*

Mere length does not impress readers.

refer

Never write *refer back.*

reinforce

religious titles

Some samples of usage:

1. *the Rev. Harvey Richards* for a priest or minister, then *Father Richards* or *Rev. Richards.*

2. *Rabbi Jason Samuel,* then *Rabbi Samuel.*

3. *Brother Juan Gomez,* then *Brother Gomez.*

4. *Sister Mary Crowley,* then *Sister Crowley.*

Never refer to a member of the clergy as just *a reverend* or *the reverend.*

See **names, titles.**

right-handed

rock 'n' roll

Rosh Hashana

ROTC

Reserve Officers' Training Corps is the denotation. See **abbreviations.**

S

said, says

Use *said* or *says.* Avoid expressions that unnecessarily color the facts or imply mind reading, such as *believed, claimed, feels* and *thinks.*

saint
Use *St.* in the names of saints, cities and schools: *St. Catherine; St. Paul, Minn.; St. Sebastian's School.*

school colors
Capitalize when synonymous with a team or school: *The Big Green bowed to the Orange and Black.*

school mascot
Capitalize: *The Tigers defeated the Hawks 43-0.*

scores
Use numerals, with hyphens between totals: *The Rams beat the Lions 14-3.* (Note absence of comma before the score.)
See **numbers.**

scuba

seasons
Lowercase: *spring, fall.*

self
Hyphenate this prefix: *self-sufficient.*

semicolon {;}
Use a semicolon
1. to separate items in a series if the items include commas: *Varsity letters went to Mike Chang, a senior; John Cummings, a junior; and Albert Williams, a sophomore.*
2. to link independent clauses when there is no coordinating conjunction: *Getting into college is one challenge; staying there is another.*
3. to link independent clauses when one of the clauses is internally punctuated: *Joe, who liked my story, wrote*

me a note; but Sheila, who can't stand sports, threw the article into the wastebasket.

See **clauses and phrases, complex and compound sentences, elections, punctuation, standard forms.**

sentence structure

The simple declarative sentence should be the basis for most news writing. Its arrangement is often subject, verb, object.

If most sentences in a story appear in this arrangement, change the pace. To add variety, place a phrase or a dependent clause before the subject of the main clause. A frequent form of inversion in news writing is object, subject, verb, with the quotation or paraphrase coming first: *"Not today," the principal said.*

shall, will

Use *shall* to express determination: *We shall win the prize.*

Use *will* in most future forms: *We will stop by our lockers after lunch.*

sic

Use this word to show you know that material you are quoting contains an error: *The newspaper said he's a member of the "Bosston City Council" [sic].*

sizable

slander

In general, this term means spoken defamation that is not provably true.

See **defamation, libel.**

sophomore

Never use *soph.*

spelling

When in doubt, look it up. The staff should use one dictionary as its standard reference.

Use the spell checker on the computer, but do not rely entirely on this program. Spell checking does not pick up homonyms, *their/they're*, *its/it's*, omissions and such inaccuracies as *form/from*.

Allow time to read over your work carefully, word by word if necessary, before you turn it in.

See **its, it's; their, there, they're.**

stacked quotations

Avoid the abrupt effect that results from running the words of several sources in succession without adequate transitions.

See **attribution, quotation.**

standard forms

So many situations recur that every publication should adopt standard forms for certain types of copy.

Metropolitan dailies carry standard forms for reporting summaries of sports events. Choose a set for various sports (baseball, football, soccer, swimming, etc.) and follow them exactly.

Note: Distinguish between English and metric units of measure, whichever is used for a particular event.

This sample portion of a track meet summary shows style for places, times, heights, distances, etc.:

100-yd. dash—1. Morton, T; 2. Tomlin, T; 3. Clark, R. Time, 10.4 sec.

880-yd. run—1. Burk, T; 2 Chase, R; 3. Wilkins, R. Time, 2 min., 15.6 sec.

High Jump—1. Gage, T; 2. Bates, R; 3. Winters, T. Height, 5 ft., 6 3/4 in.

Long Jump—1. Bates, H; 2. Walters, R; 3. Jenkins, T. Distance, 19 ft. 7 5/8 in.

One Mile Relay—1. Trenton (Moberly, Pizer, Zagalis), 2. Rahway (Simpson, Husker, Clarke, Jones). Time, 3 min., 28.6 sec.

states and commonwealths

In the United States there are 46 states; there are four commonwealths: Kentucky, Massachusetts, Pennsylvania and Virginia. Except in formal uses, refer to all 50 as states.

Guidelines:

1. Do not capitalize *commonwealth of* or *state of.*

2. Capitalize and write out states' names when they stand alone.

3. Abbreviate when state name appears with name of county or municipality: *Dade County, Fla., Mineola, N.Y.*

4. Be consistent.

Abbreviations may be in standard U.S. Postal Service form with two letters capitalized: *Alabama becomes AL; Alaska, AK; Arizona, AZ; Arkansas, AR; California, CA; Colorado, CO; Connecticut, CT; Delaware, DE; Florida, FL; Georgia, GA; Hawaii, HI; Idaho, ID; Illinois, IL; Indiana, IN; Iowa, IA; Kansas, KS; Kentucky, KY; Louisiana, LA; Maine, ME; Maryland, MD; Massachusetts, MA; Michigan, MI; Minnesota, MN; Mississippi, MS; Missouri, MO; Montana, MT; Nebraska, NE; Nevada, NV; New Hampshire, NH; New Jersey, NJ; New Mexico, NM; New York, NY; North Carolina, NC; North Dakota, ND; Ohio, OH; Oklahoma, OK; Oregon, OR; Pennsylvania, PA; Rhode Island, RI; South Carolina, SC; South Dakota, SD; Tennessee, TN; Texas, TX; Utah, UT; Vermont, VT; Virginia, VA; Washington, WA; West Virginia, WV; Wisconsin, WI; Wyoming, WY.*

Most news publications, however, use the following: *Ala., Ariz., Ark., Calif., Colo., Conn., Del., Fla., Ga., Ill., Ind., Kan., Ky., La., Md., Mass., Mich., Minn., Miss., Mo., Mont., Neb., Nev., N.H., N.J., N.M., N.Y., N.C., N.D., Okla., Ore., Pa., R.I., S.C., S.D., Tenn., Vt., Va., Wash., W. Va., Wis., Wyo.*

Note that in this style *Alaska, Hawaii, Idaho, Iowa, Maine, Ohio, Texas* and *Utah* are not abbreviated.

See **addresses.**

stationary, stationery

Stationary, an adjective, means staying in one place: *Sit in a stationary position.*

Stationery, a noun, means writing paper and envelopes. *Try this stationery for your job application.*

stepfather, stepmother

subcommittee

subhead

Use subheads below a main headline and within a story to add emphasis and create white space.

For a subhead that appears directly below the main headline, use contrasting, smaller type. This subhead should be about the width of the main headline.

When subheads set off main sections in longer stories, use display type or boldface type.

See **headline, kicker.**

subjunctive

Use subjunctive for conditions contrary to fact, and for strong doubts, regrets and wishes: *If I were the principal, I would support an ice hockey team. I wish it were possible to fund an ice hockey program.*

But: *If John Brown becomes principal, he expects to*

support an ice hockey team. He said he hoped it would be possible to fund an ice hockey program.

superintendent

suppose, supposed
Use *suppose* to express conjecture: *I suppose we'd better go to practice.*
Use *supposed* to express obligation: *We're supposed to be at practice on time.*

syllabication
Consult the dictionary the staff has adopted. In general, avoid dividing words.
Some guidelines:
1. Never divide proper nouns, abbreviations, numbers, addresses or dates, contractions, or words of fewer than six letters.
2. Divide by syllable near the middle of a word.
3. Avoid confusing divisions, such as *un-iverse.*
4. Put the hyphen at the end of the line, not the beginning.
If you are using a word processor, see if it has a syllabication feature.
See **hyphen.**

T

teachers, faculty, staff
Teachers are part of the *faculty,* which includes counselors and administrators. The *faculty* is part of the *staff,* which includes cafeteria workers, custodians and secretaries.

team
A team is a collective noun that takes a singular verb

and matches a singular pronoun: *The baseball team will host its major rival this afternoon.*

teen-age, teen-ager

temperature
Use numerals except for zero: *95-degree heat, temperatures in the 70s, 10 below zero.*

that, which
Use *that* for references to inanimate objects and animals in essential clauses and phrases: *School publications that are full of important news enlighten readers.*
Use *which* for nonessential clauses and phrases: *School publications, which are full of important news, enlighten readers.*
Never use *that* or *which* for people; use *who: All the students who are in my class are going to the presentation.*
Not: *All the students that are in my class are going to the presentation.*
See **clauses and phrases; comma; who, whom.**

their, there, they're
Use these homonyms correctly: *They won their award in the Science Olympiad. There's a moon out tonight. They're all in the lecture hall.*

this
Use *this* as an adjective: *This discussion with the administration will prevent confusion.*
Do not use *this* as a pronoun: *This will prevent confusion.*

titles
These words and phrases exactly define a person's

official, professional scope of authority: *principal, senator, superintendent.*

Distinguish between false titles and formal titles.

1. Capitalize one-word formal titles that precede a person's name: *Mayor Janet McDermott, Queen Victoria.*

2. Use lowercase for formal titles that follow a name or stand alone: *Janet McDermott, mayor; the mayor.*

3. Do not separate a one-word formal title that precedes a name and the name with a comma: *President Bill Clinton.*

Not: *President, Bill Clinton.*

4. Place formal titles consisting of several words after the name: *David Smith, the history and social sciences department head, decided to set up the exchange.*

5. Use consistent forms for titles of books, CDs, lectures, magazine or newspaper articles, movies, operas, periodicals, plays, poems, speeches, television programs and works of art.

Capitalize all initial letters in the first and last words of a title and in all other words except articles, conjunctions and prepositions of three or fewer letters: *"In the Still of the Night."*

Some publications enclose all titles with quotation marks. Others drop the quotation marks and may use italics for titles of books, movies periodicals, plays, operas and television programs.

Avoid long lists of titles set off in quotation marks. For example: *They listened to Beethoven's String Quartet in F major, Op. 59, No. 1; to Haydn's String Quartet in E flat major, Op. 76, No. 6; and to Mozart's Symphony in C (Jupiter), K.-V. 551.*

See **boldface and italics, courtesy titles, false titles, political titles, quotation marks, religious titles.**

tobacco

total, totaled, totaling

transfer, transferred, transferring

try to
Use *try to.* Never write *try and.*

typography
Ideally, the size and weight of the display type used for a headline correspond to the story's importance. Headline sizes are expressed in points. There are 72 points to the inch. Weight refers to the degree of boldness of the type.
Here is a general guide for type characters' unit values. Each lowercase letter and each space between words normally count one unit, except m and w, which count one-and-a-half, and f, l ,i, t, j, which count one-half. Most punctuation counts one-half. Uppercase letters count one-and-a-half, except M and W, which count two, and I, which counts one.

U

ultra
In general, no hyphen: *ultrasound.*

un
In general, no hyphen: *uncover.*

unique
Do not use *very* with *unique,* which means one of a kind.

United States
Write it out as a noun. U.S. may be used as an adjective.
See **America.**

up

Do not use as a verb, as in *The team upped its record.* Choose a better word: *improved, raised,* etc.

used to

Used to is past tense: *I used to hear people say, "Go find her near the lockers."*

V

versus

Write *vs.* in sports references, as in *Pope John vs. Holy Name;* write *v.* when citing a legal case: *Roe v. Wade.*

very, really, actually

Avoid these overused adverbs and others like them. Find a more precise way to express an idea.

Veterans Day

vice president

Do not hyphenate.

W-Z

war

Capitalize when part of a name: *World War II.*

weather, whether

Use accurately: *I don't know whether the weather will be sunny.*

weights

Use numerals: *the 8-pound, 6-ounce boy.*

weird
See **"i" before "e."**

who, whom
Use *who* for subjects or predicate nominatives as you would use *he, she, they: Anne Baker, who should make the all-star team, is a junior. Who will make the all-star team?*
Use *whom* for objects, as you would use *him, her, them: Anne Baker, whom the coach called "a player with great potential," should make the all-star team.*
See **pronouns; that, which.**

Xerox
Do not use this brand name as a synonym for photocopier.
See **brand names.**

Yom Kippur

zero, zeros

ZIP code

PLAGIARISM

Presenting someone else's creation as one's own
by Mike Hiestand

"Plagiarist!" It is an accusation that strikes fear in the hearts of students, academics, journalists, authors and presidential candidates alike.

The fear is certainly that of being caught: punished by those in authority, professionally censured by one's peers, publicly humiliated. Often too, however, it is a fear of the unknown.

From the day a 3rd-grade student is assigned a report on Thomas Jefferson and turns to an encyclopedia, he confronts the same questions that face a best-selling historian who dares consult secondary sources: How do I use this information without "overusing" it? How much use is too much? What needs to be attributed and what doesn't? Is substantially rewording or paraphrasing a passage sufficient to make it one's own? What constitutes "substantially"? And on and on. Even when one makes every conscious effort to avoid the P-word, the nagging thought can remain: What if it wasn't enough?

Plagiarism is a scary topic for many because it is a moving topic. A gray topic. An unknown. Everybody wants a simple definition of plagiarism. The problem is, there isn't one. In fact, there are many definitions of plagiarism. The American Association of University Professors, the American Historical Association, the Associated Collegiate Press—all, to name just a few, have their own definitions of plagiarism—and none of them is especially simple to understand, or moreover, to apply.

For example, in a widely reported case, the AHA investigated the historian Stephen B. Oates on charges that he plagiarized his biographies of William Faulkner, Martin Luther King Jr., and Nat Turner.

Oates was also accused of plagiarism by government whistle blowers who had used a computer text-analyzing machine to identify hundreds of passages in Oates' work that contained words or phrases similar to those used in the works of other authors, an investigatory practice that set off a controversy all its own.

For example, the computer came up with the two following passages:

From *Time* magazine February 18, 1957: "Up to 25 profanity-laced telephone calls a day came to the King home. Sometimes there was only the hawk of a throat and the splash of spittle against the earpiece."

From Oates' 1982 book, *Let the Trumpet Sound: The Life of Martin Luther King, Jr.*: "Then there were the obscene phone calls—as many as twenty-five a day now. Sometimes there was only the hawk of a throat, the sound of spit against the receiver."

The AHA's written decision met wide criticism for creating more questions than it answered. In the decision, the association found "no evidence that Stephen Oates committed plagiarism as it is conventionally understood." The report, however, went on to say that the AHA had found "evidence in Mr. Oates' work of too great and too continuous dependence, even with attribution, on the structure, distinctive language and rhetorical strategies of other scholars and sources." Oates, like many others, has called the finding "incredibly vague."

And it is. But then so is the definition—or definitions—on which the AHA relied. In May, 1993, the AHA revised its plagiarism policy. Before that, it defined plagiarism more broadly as "the expropriation of another author's findings, interpretation, or text, presented thereafter as one's own creation without proper attribution to its actual source."

The AHA now defines plagiarism simply as "the expropriation of another author's text, and the presentation of it as one's own." The new policy also contains a second category of offenses called "misuse," which includes "the limited borrowing, without attribution, of another's distinctive and significant research findings, hypothesis, theories...or interpretations."

As the Oates case apparently points out, however, simple word counts or computer-driven comparisons are incapable of sufficiently weighing the nuances and complexities that each case potentially brings.

Plagiarism is not a legal term. As noted above, it is a term for an academic crime, usually defined by professional or academic bodies. There are no civil statutes, accompanied by legal definition, that one can look to for guidance. Indeed, the amount of guidance available will vary depending on the specific definition one uses and on the body responsible for investigating the charges.

You won't be tossed in jail or fined by a state or federal court if you are found guilty of plagiarizing someone else's work. But you might be subject to punishment or censure by a non-legal body with the ability to enforce its findings.

In addition, most publications have policies against plagiarism, and reporters have occasionally been fired by their employers for improperly using another's work.

Copyright law—for which a body of federal law does exist and whose violation can result in civil fines or other penalties—is a cousin of plagiarism, but with a few key differences.

Simply stated, a plagiarist is a person who poses as the creator of words, ideas or methods that are not his own.

In contrast, a person infringes on another's copyright when he makes *unauthorized use* of material that is protected by copyright.

A few distinctions stand out.

First, for purposes of plagiarism, the material someone has stolen need not have the protection of copyright. For example, a person could plagiarize Shakespeare's works by not giving The Bard proper credit. He would not, however, be guilty of copyright infringement because all of Shakespeare's works, now approximately 400 years old, are in the public domain and can't be protected by copyright.

Second, a copyright violation can occur even though the infringer gives proper credit to the creator and is, therefore, not guilty of plagiarism. For example, a student newspaper cannot, without permission, lift a picture out of *Newsweek* to illustrate its own story—even if the source of the photo is carefully identified.

Of course, some people simultaneously take credit for and improperly use the work of others. They are both plagiarists and copyright infringers.

Despite the ambiguity that can exist during a formal investigation of a charge of plagiarism, there are a few guidelines that can help conscientious students, teachers and others from falling into the plagiarism pit in the first place. Anne H. Frank, counsel to the American Association of University Professors, has pointed out the following:

First, almost all definitions of plagiarism require *intent* on the part of the alleged plagiarist. In other words, sloppy scholarship or sloppy journalism alone is not sufficient to sustain a charge of plagiarism. The plagiarist must have intended to deceive others into thinking that the copied work was, in fact, his own.

Second, the form of the text is relevant.

"Verbatim copying, without quotation marks or attribution, is generally more offensive than the paraphrase," Frank says.

Similarly, she points out in the September-October, 1993 issue of *Academe* that the context in which the original work is used is relevant to the determination or at least the severity of a plagiarism charge.

For example, a student taking an Ellen Goodman column from *The Boston Globe* and running it in the student newspaper under her own name, as one adviser called recently to tell me one of his students had done, is different from a student inserting a paragraph from that column, without proper attribution, in an otherwise creative 200-page thesis. Both examples are plagiarism though most would agree the degree of the offense differs.

A third suggestion is to "adequately"—read "frequently"—cite the earlier source in the later work.

This last suggestion points out what is probably the most important thing to keep in mind to avoid getting caught in the plagiarism tangle: When in doubt about how to use material in some way derived from someone else's hard work, simply attribute it. Don't chance it.

Understanding and, moreover, defending against a charge of plagiarism can be a confusing and complicated process.

While some cases are so blatant that no defense is possible, most are "in disguise," requiring significant effort to adequately and fairly address the various nuances or shades that are hallmarks of the creative process. The results can be messy. Cautious and deliberate avoidance is the best—and only—defense.

Mike Hiestand is an attorney with the Student Press Law Center. The center provides free legal counsel to high school and college student journalists and their advisers around the country. The address is Suite 1910, 1101 Wilson Blvd., Arlington, Va. 22209.

INDEX

COPYEDITING MARKS

Everyone who writes and edits for the publication should learn the following symbols:

L	Beginning a paragraph.
¶	Begin paragraph.
feature ends/	No paragraph.
Bring it (Run in)	Run in. Set material in continuous paragraph.
No¶	No paragraph.
(August 3)	Abbreviate or spell out as the case may be.
cafe	Set in boldface or italics.
Times	Set in capitals and small capitals.
thomas	Make it a capital.
Street	Reduce capital to lower case.
per son	Close up space.
see that	Leave a space between words.
to soon go	Transpose the enclosed elements.
I also asked	Bridge line carries over deleted material.
x or ⊙	Period.
,	Comma.
# or xxx	Placed at the end of the article to show ending.
he asked when	Marks point where insertion is made.

PROOFREADING

The proofreader reads and corrects the printed proof.

The marks given below are the standard proofreading marks in use in most printing establishments.

ABBREVIATION

spell out	Substitute full spelling of a word or number.
fig	Substitute figures.

PARAGRAPH

¶	Begin new paragraph.
No¶	Do not begin new paragraph.
Run in	Make elements follow in same line without a break.

INSERTION OR OMISSION

∧	Indicates point of omission
∫	Take out part marked.
Stet	Do not make change indicated. In addition to this mark in the margin, a set of dots is placed under the words in question.